This Book Belongs To:

_____

Jasmine
The Golden Key

DISNEY PRESS

New York

Early one morning, the Sultan summoned Jasmine and Aladdin to his grand throne room. "Today I'm leaving Agrabah to go visit an old friend," he said. "In my absence, the two of you will be in charge."

Jasmine smiled. "We'll do our very best, father," she said.

Suddenly, a loud shriek came from above. Abu, the cheeky little monkey, was flying around on the Magic Carpet.

"Abu!" Aladdin cried. "Get down here, please."

But Abu didn't obey. He was having too much fun! The Sultan raised an eyebrow at the mischievous monkey.

A little while later, the Sultan was ready to leave. "Don't forget that you will be receiving foreign ambassadors tomorrow," he reminded Jasmine.

"Ambassadors!" the princess cried. Her eyes grew wide.

"Don't worry, dear," the Sultan assured her. "You'll do fine. I know you will."

"Of course we will," Aladdin chimed in, smiling confidently.

Before riding out of the palace gate, the Sultan handed Jasmine a large golden key. "This is the key to the palace and all of its riches," he said. "Take good care of it."

Jasmine nodded. Just then, they heard Rajah the tiger growling loudly. Abu was at it again! The silly monkey had pulled Rajah's tail. But all of a sudden, the shiny key caught Abu's eye, and he lost interest in teasing Rajah.

As soon as the Sultan was gone, Aladdin was ready to have some fun. "We have the whole place to ourselves!" he exclaimed. "Let's enjoy life a little."

But Jasmine wanted to make sure everything was ready for the ambassadors' reception. She handed the golden key to Aladdin and went to check on the guest wing. Aladdin trailed after her.

In the guest room, Aladdin threw himself on a bed, tossing the golden key into the air. "Come on, we've watched your father receive ambassadors a million times," he said. "There's nothing to it."

Jasmine ignored him and hurried out of the room.

Meanwhile, an annoyed Rajah had been chasing Abu through the guest wing, making a terrible mess.

A few moments later, Aladdin drifted off to sleep on the comfortable bed. When he woke up, he wandered up to the roof terrace for some lunch.

By then, Jasmine had spent an hour talking to the chef. She wanted the ambassadors to have a delicious feast. They had just decided on the menu when they heard a loud crash.

Jasmine and the chef ran down into the storeroom, and guess who they found? Rajah. And he was surrounded by broken jars and spilled cooking oils!

Jasmine spent half an hour trying to rinse the oil out of Rajah's fur. Without a murmur, the embarrassed tiger let her splash water over him until he was all clean.

Later at dinner, the princess looked solemnly at Aladdin. "My father has shown us great trust by letting us be in charge of the palace and receive the ambassadors tomorrow."

Aladdin nodded in agreement.

"So, please, all of you," Jasmine continued, looking at Abu, Rajah, and Aladdin, "help me get everything ready. I know my father would want the palace to be sparkling and shiny."

Abu's eyes lit up. The little monkey just loved things that sparkled and shined.

"Where is the golden key?" Jasmine asked Aladdin after dinner. "I need to get into the treasury."

"The key . . . eh . . ." Aladdin began. "I don't remember."

Everyone searched the palace, but the key was nowhere to be found.

"We'll find it. Don't worry!" Aladdin promised. "Tomorrow you will continue the preparations for the reception, and Abu, Rajah, and I will find the key."

The next morning, they all set to work—except Abu. Aladdin tried to wake up the monkey, but it was useless. He was snoring loudly beneath the Magic Carpet, who seemed just as exhausted.

Suddenly, Aladdin heard a cry from down in the courtyard. He rushed over to the balcony, looked down, and saw gold coins spraying out of the fountain!

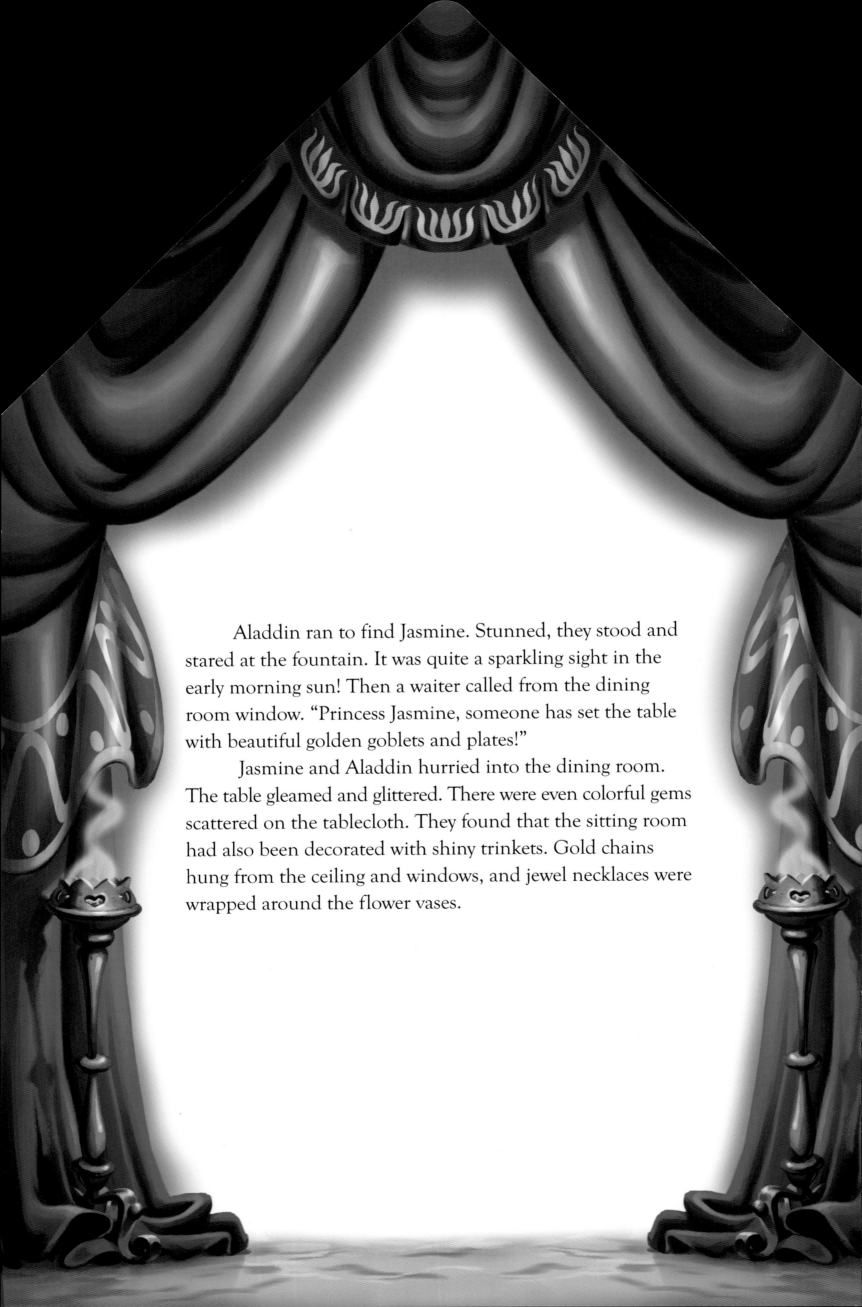

Aladdin ran to find Jasmine. Stunned, they stood and stared at the fountain. It was quite a sparkling sight in the early morning sun! Then a waiter called from the dining room window. "Princess Jasmine, someone has set the table with beautiful golden goblets and plates!"

Jasmine and Aladdin hurried into the dining room. The table gleamed and glittered. There were even colorful gems scattered on the tablecloth. They found that the sitting room had also been decorated with shiny trinkets. Gold chains hung from the ceiling and windows, and jewel necklaces were wrapped around the flower vases.

Jasmine wasn't pleased when she looked into the throne room. But Aladdin couldn't help giggling. "Look at the statues' funny hairdos!"

Taking a deep breath, Jasmine tried to stay calm. "I know I said my father would want the palace to be sparkling and shiny," she said, "but this is not what I meant."

Then Jasmine ran down to the treasury beneath the throne room. The door had been left open, and the room was almost empty!

"Someone has been busy," Aladdin said as he caught up with the princess. "Hmm, that someone must also be very exhausted. I think I know who it was!"

Startled, the Magic Carpet rose into the air as Aladdin shook Abu awake. And there, right next to the monkey, lay the golden key.

"You little thief!" Aladdin cried. "You've made a mess of the whole palace."

"Well," Jasmine said, "he did try to make it sparkle and shine."

Abu nodded and scowled at Aladdin.

Your nap is over," Aladdin snapped. "Abu, you and the Magic Carpet will help tidy up. We have no time to spare." Quickly, they all began bringing the gold coins and chains, gold bars, jewels, and gems back down into the treasury.

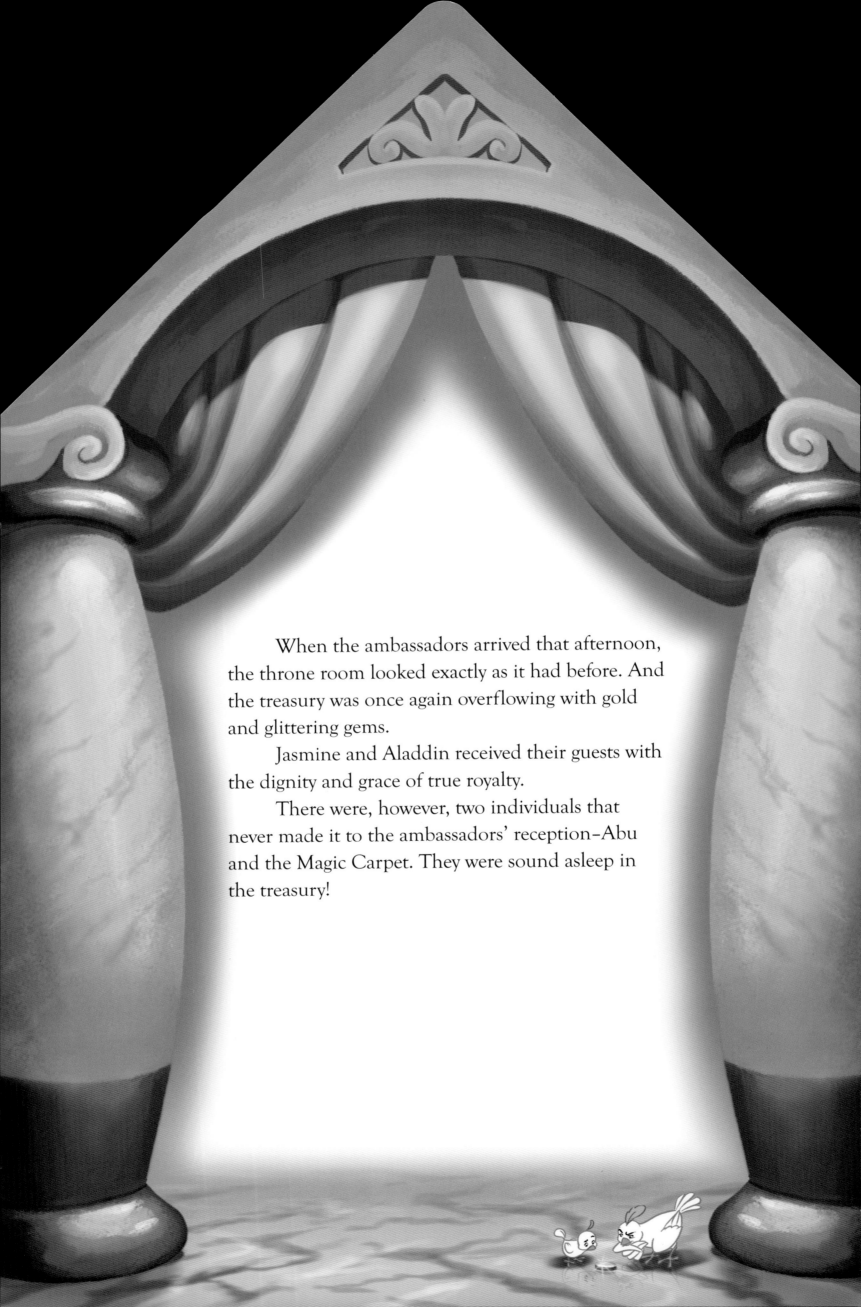

When the ambassadors arrived that afternoon, the throne room looked exactly as it had before. And the treasury was once again overflowing with gold and glittering gems.

Jasmine and Aladdin received their guests with the dignity and grace of true royalty.

There were, however, two individuals that never made it to the ambassadors' reception—Abu and the Magic Carpet. They were sound asleep in the treasury!

Unfortunately, Abu didn't get the pleasure of watching
the ambassadors *ooh* and *aah* at the beautifully set dining table.
Jasmine had decided to leave the golden plates and goblets
to celebrate her and Aladdin's first ambassador reception.

Even though the monkey had made a mess of things,
Jasmine had given him the golden key to guard during dinner.
After all, Abu had proved that he was good at looking after
the key—even Aladdin had to admit that!

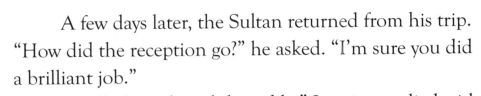

A few days later, the Sultan returned from his trip. "How did the reception go?" he asked. "I'm sure you did a brilliant job."

"Well, the palace did sparkle," Jasmine replied with a smile.

Aladdin nodded and snapped his fingers for Abu to return the golden key to the Sultan. Abu hesitated at first—he would miss the shiny treasure!—but at last he obeyed. After all, Agrabah was full of beautiful things for a cheeky little monkey.